Millionaire Manager

"A smart approach to financial management. As essential to success as a good business plan."
— Philip E. Harriman, Chartered Financial Consultant,
Former Maine State Senator

"Congratulations on writing a book on understanding finance that is simple and effective."
— Jean Otte, Founder & CEO Women Unlimited

"I've been to over 13 YPO Universities and the best resource I have ever encountered was Curt Symonds."
— Dorset White, CEO, Tork, Inc.

"Yours is the kind of course that has real, practical, take-home value, and we can't get enough of that type of training."
— Jack W. Poole, CEO, Daon Development Corporation

"Congratulations! It looks like you have accomplished the difficult task of putting theoretical concepts into the practical language which the businessman needs and appreciates."
— Donald A. Press, Associate Dean for Academic Programs,
Boston University

"The new knowledge that Curt Symonds has provided me is challenging my past habits and providing me with a more effective and plain old smart way to analyze our businesses..."
— John Hart, Controller

"I found Mr. Symonds' talks to be among the most valuable educational experiences that I have had in some twenty odd years of post education."
— Rev. John F.X. Sheehan, Marquette University

"Since first attending Curt Symonds' Financial Management Seminars, we have been able to take this company from a low return on investment before taxes and interest to a Return on Investment before taxes and interest that places us securely in the top ten of Forbes Magazine's latest 'last 12 months' list of High Return on Capital Companies. Management here owes Curt Symonds no small debt for his contribution to its techniques."
— C.R. Mallory Smith, President, Koppers International

"Curtis Symonds' book, "Profit Dollars and Earnings Sense" shows us a means of putting each of the profit measurements commonly used in business into proper perspective – aimed at achieving not only a more complete understanding, but hopefully, a better management of the profit system under which business operates."
— John Budlong, (former) President,
American Management Association

MILLIONAIRE MANAGER ROIC CASE STUDIES

SMALL BUSINESS

Challenge: Small, profitable manufacturer earning $3,000,000 in sales. Owner wishing to pursue other interests wanted to sell the company.
Solution: Hired Curt Symonds to consult. Using Return on Invested Capital (ROIC) techniques, the owner brought his business back to a stable cash position and sold his company two years later for $7,000,000 plus a ten year bonus plan.
Outcome: The new owner kept the ROIC measurements in place, and working with Curt Symonds quarterly, the company weathered economic and industry downswings, diversified, and 18 years later the company was sold for $58,000,000.

MIDDLE MARKET

Challenge: Privately held company doing $600M in sales, with four diverse divisions in supermarkets, media, automotive and publishing, 8,000 employees, needed a way to measure the profitability of their divisions.
Solution: Hired Curt Symonds to consult and teach division managers the concepts of ROIC measurements which became the cornerstone philosophy of running and measuring their business.
Outcome: Sales increased and total assets improved, with the side benefit that the company performed satisfactorily against a deteriorating North American economy in the early 90's.
Using ROIC measurements and techniques, this company grew from $600 million in sales to $2.5 billion in 19 years and now stands at $5.5 billion, eight divisions, 25,000 employees.

FORTUNE 500

Challenge: A Fortune 500 company was earning a low return on its capital and needed to improve its operating results.
Solution: Attended Curt Symonds' Financial Management seminars and in consultations with Mr. Symonds, implemented Return on Invested Capital techniques, company wide.
Outcome: Using Curt Symonds' techniques, this company improved it's earnings and was listed in Forbes Top Ten High Return on Capital companies.

Millionaire Manager

Curtis W. Symonds
Carole A. Symonds, CPA, MST

Global Financial Publishing
Portland, Maine

© 2005 Global Financial Publishing
and Carole A. Symonds
All rights reserved.

The Millionaire Manager and the Millionaire Manager logo are trademarks of Global Financial Publishing, registered to the U.S. and other countries.

While this book is intended to provide timely and accurate information regarding the subjects discussed, it should not be used as a substitute for professional advice. This book is intended to provide general guidance only. In some cases, the information provided in this book may not apply to you. Accordingly, do not take any action or otherwise rely on this book without first seeking advice from a skilled financial, tax, legal or other professional advisor. You should not infer any guarantees or warranties of any kind from any sales representatives or sales materials, and the author and the publisher each disclaim any and all warranties of any kind in regards to this book and the information provided herein, including, without limitation, any implied warranties of merchantability and fitness for a particular purpose

This book is protected by United States and international copyright laws. You may not reproduce or create derivative works based on this book (or any portions thereof) in any form or by any means without the prior written permission of the author and the publisher.

Library of Congress Catalog No. 2003103178
ISBN 0-9631056-4-7
Includes Glossary and Index

Published in the United States of America
Global Financial Publishing

www.MillionaireManager.com

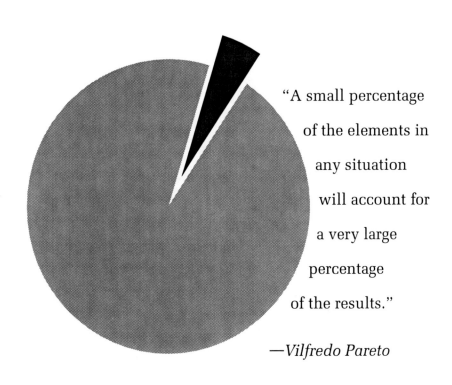

"A small percentage of the elements in any situation will account for a very large percentage of the results."

—*Vilfredo Pareto*

DEDICATION

This book is dedicated to my father, who pioneered the use of return on invested capital throughout countless companies and organizations around the world, helping those business owners and managers increase their profitability through better financial management tools. He was the greatest teacher I ever had, and his ability to communicate complex economic and financial issues in comprehensive simple terms has been an inspiration to me in my own career. This book is the result of his vision, his dream, and his legacy. I love you, Dad.

ACKNOWLEDGMENTS

This book would not be complete without thanking my mentors and colleagues who have encouraged my career every step of the way... Rich Calzaretta, Mike Carona, Jim Connor, Mike Costello, Gain Francis, Jay Mattie, Annette Smith and Bob Zarzar – I owe you no small debt of gratitude. Also, my sincere thanks to: John Allam, Bita Alu, Jamie Alu, Otis Anderson, Steve Appe, Roberta Arendt, Brian Atchinson, Jim Banks, Lin Bell, Rick Berry, Shay Blanchette, Tom Casey, Joe Castriano, Carolyn Canova, Jim Cavallo, Peter Clarke, John Clymer, Brian Cornell, Bernadette Crehan, Cosmo DeStefano, Dick Dubois, Sasha Durand, Mark Dionne, Tim Egan, Siobhan Fulton, Stephen Goeben, Margo Green, Greg Grobstein, Jamie Grow, Mike Hardgrove, Phil Harriman, Chip Harter, Tom Holly, Kelly Horn, Tana Hulse, Fiona Hunter, Dan Hutchins, Steve Jacques, Marty Janowiecki, Paul Joubert, John Lane, Fred Lipp, Andy Macwilliam, Debbie McKie, Vicki Meyer, Mike Morrow, Andrew Murray-Brown, Dan Nelson, Don Nowill, John O'Connor, Barry Okun, Ted Ousback, John Overpeck, Greg Parinello, Rich Pattenaude, Mick Penizotto, Sari Rapkin, Lynne Reeder, Wayne Robinson, Don Rocen, Mark Rovnak, Mary Shumaker, Tony Smith, Rick Stamm, Rich Stovsky, Thomas "Sully" Sullivan, John Tam, Jim Tapper, Lisa Tassinari, Bob Valletta, Lynn Waespi, Glenn Williams, Brett Yacker, and David Zimmerman.

There are no words to thank the wonderful artistic and publishing talent who made this book possible: Rowan Bishop, Bob Cott, Joline Gilman, Gregory Heald, Deborah Leighton, Nathan Sanborn, Linda Spring, and the WordCo team.

From my heart... Carole

Preface

The new millennium has brought many changes to the financial world. Gone is the bull market of the late 1990s where everything connected to the Internet turned to gold. The technology boom and e-business craze tested the theory that a company's value could be based solely on revenue or "click-throughs" (a measurement of traffic on a company's website). Surprise. It was proven once again that, at the end of the day, investors require a return on their money. Even in this new world, the old rules still apply. Companies need to earn a reasonable profit to stay competitive and attract new investment dollars.

So what is the concept of profit? How do you determine a reasonable profit for an amount invested? Are two companies that have a five percent return on sales equally profitable? No. You can't simply look to the reported net earnings on the income statement to determine a company's profitability. To truly measure profit, you need to have an understanding of what profit is and how much capital was invested in the business to earn that profit.

Let me dispel one misconception right now. You don't have to be an accountant to understand profit. In fact, accounting rules have no connection to and make no attempt at measuring economic profitability. The purpose of Generally Accepted Accounting Principles (GAAP) is to develop consistent rules to match the timing of when revenue and expenses are recorded so that financial data is more comparable and reliable across organizations. GAAP was never designed to measure a company's value or determine an appropriate return for the risks assumed by the business owners and other stakeholders. With the continued use of accounting statements and accounting terminology as the source for measuring profits, managers and business owners have adopted a technician's view of profit as a remainder amount. Being "in the black" has equated to being profitable. This reliance on accounting principles as a profit measurement is not only misleading, its continued use could cause a company to steadily lose value while its accounting "profits" are increasing.

To give you an example, in one of the country's largest bankruptcies, WorldCom hid expenses from its investors by capitalizing costs as an asset on its balance sheet. By doing so, WorldCom was able to keep these expenses off the income statement, thereby inflating the "profits" reported to the market. This, in turn, increased WorldCom's earnings per share (EPS). The techniques in this book would have shown that WorldCom was steadily losing value even as it was reporting profits to its investors.[1]

In this book, we have taken the concepts of Return on Invested Capital and laid them out in a step-by-step approach that is easy for any manager or business owner to understand and apply to their own business. By following these techniques, you will understand the relationship between earnings, capital employed, and cost of capital and how this relationship impacts your business's true profitability. Apply these concepts to your company, your division, your product line, or your personal investments[2] and get an accurate profit measurement from which you can make better business decisions.

---

[1] During the period 1998–2001, WorldCom went from reporting a loss per share of ($1.35) to reporting an earnings per share high of $1.46. During this same period, WorldCom's Return on Invested Capital decreased from 8.2% to a low of 2.6%. Further, between 1999 and 2000, the company reported an increase in net earnings of 5.6%. But during that same period, capital increased by 6.6%, so the earnings "growth" wasn't really growth at all; the earnings had to increase just to support the additional capital being utilized in the business.

[2] For a more detailed discussion of applying Return on Invested Capital to your investment portfolio, the authors refer you to *The Millionaire Manager Talks to Wall Street*.

Millionaire Manager

It began as a trickle, turned into a flood, and quickly became a deluge. The monthly reports became weekly…and then hourly printouts…printouts with endless listings of the detail of every conceivable aspect of the business.

And once the detail became the norm, management began to absorb it and soon knew more and more about less and less.

The computer had given us the Information Age…and with it far more "information" than we needed to know.

I looked for a better way and that's when I met…

The Millionaire Manager…

I first met the man in a small town I visited from time to time. I noticed him because he stood out from the crowd, because he had succeeded where others had failed.

What he had done, quite simply, was to start a small business, manage it well, and enable it to grow slowly and steadily over the years. He had stayed the course while many others had come and gone. I asked him about it, about what he knew that the others didn't.

He smiled. "A lot of people ask me that same question. It's quite simple, really. I manage by my rule of *five percent*. In fact, some folks around here call me the five percent manager," he replied, as he leaned back in his chair.

I was intrigued.

"Does that mean you have a five percent profit?" I asked, thinking he must be referring to the usual meaning most managers had when speaking of percentages in their business.

"Not at all!" was his amused answer. "Although that does seem to be the accepted wisdom with most people. No, my *five percent management* is a lot different. It all started with the story that probably brought you here in the first place — why I'm still here and most of the others are not."

"You mean you just learned from their mistakes and then managed to avoid them? To do things differently?"

"You might put it that way," he agreed, reaching for paper and pencil on an otherwise clean desk, one which I had noticed was devoid of the usual assortment of files, memos, and reports. "And, yes, I did indeed learn quite a bit from what went wrong with their businesses and have been able to avoid some of the more obvious mistakes."

"But where does the five percent come in?" I persisted. "Were you simply five percent more profitable than the others, or what?"

The Millionaire Manager smiled again as he wrote on the paper in front of him. "No, it wasn't that, at least not in the beginning. In fact, I was probably headed in the same direction as the rest of the crowd before I began to notice something. Do you see these three numbers?" he asked, passing me a sheet of paper on which he had written in large print...

Success in Business

100% Start

95% Fail

5% Survive

"Well, that's where it started, when I found out that ninety-five percent of the other fellows didn't make it over the first ten years. They had failed one way or another — gone bankrupt, been bought out, or just closed up shop and walked away. I was a five percent survivor."

"So that's what you mean by five percent management, just being one of the five percent still in business at the end of ten years? But that's not a formula for managing your business, just a statistic of sorts. Maybe you were just luckier than the rest," I protested, a bit disappointed by his answer.

"Yes, it could have been just luck," he admitted, "if I had stopped there. But, as I said, that was simply where it all started. It was the other five percent that made the whole thing work."

"The other five percent?" I interrupted, sensing that now he might be getting to the point that had puzzled me.

"Well, as I said, I did spend quite a bit of time studying what the ninety-five percent managers may have done wrong. I talked to many of them, asked a lot of questions, and made quite a few notes."

"And what did they do wrong?" I asked, thinking that he must have uncovered quite a long list of mistakes.

"Nothing, according to their stories. It was just bad luck as they saw it. With one, it was a high inventory that tied up most of his cash; another complained of a slow collection of accounts due from his customers; a third couldn't get a loan from the bank...and so on. The list ran to some one hundred bits and pieces they blamed for losing their business. I went over the list time and again until it finally dawned on me. It all boiled down to one common problem."

"And that was...?" I prodded impatiently.

"TOO MUCH DETAIL!" the Millionaire Manager replied quickly, now leaning forward in his chair in a more urgent manner. "Entirely too much detail! They had a hundred pieces of the puzzle but no way to put it all together. They weren't running the business; it was running them. They were so busy counting the trees they couldn't see the forest," he concluded with a shrug.

"So you simply eliminated some of the detail in running your own business?"

"Some? I eliminated ninety-five percent of it. That's where the other five percent comes in. They were handling details while I wanted to manage results. To do it, I simply boiled the list of one hundred details down to five essential elements…five percent of the total."

"Let me see if I understand you," I said eagerly.

A

Five Percent Manager

becomes a

Five Percent Survivor

in business

simply by

managing only five percent of all the detail involved in operating a business.

I thought over what I had just learned and asked, "But is it really that simple?"

The Millionaire Manager smiled.

"Yes, it's just that simple in concept, but of course you must learn what the five percent consists of as well as the sequence in which these steps must be planned and controlled," he asserted. "Once you do that, it's not much of a secret."

"Where do you begin?" I asked, impatient to learn the Millionaire Manager's five percent formula.

"Well, let's start with the two reports that most managers get in a business…the Balance Sheet and the Income Statement. The Balance Sheet, of course, lists all the things you own: the Cash, Inventory, Equipment, and so on, as well as all of the amounts you owe to your suppliers or to the bank. It also shows how much Capital you have put into the business and where it came from. It can be a very lengthy document. The Income Statement tells you how much your income has been for a period of time…what all of your costs and expenses have been and how much is left over as Profit on the bottom line. Most managers start with the Income Statement. I start with the Balance Sheet. I find it is the more important of the two in the long run. It's also the one that most managers pay the least attention to. Now, I apply my five percent rule to each of these reports, but let's begin with the Balance Sheet. The most important item on this report is the amount of Capital employed in the business."

"Exactly what is *Capital* in business?" I asked, wanting to make sure I understood all of his terminology correctly.

"Very simply, it is *the amount of money that someone has put up to get the business started and to allow it to continue and grow.* In the beginning, it is usually all supplied by the owners and is called *Equity Capital*. Later, as time goes on, *Debt Capital* will probably be added as the business borrows money from the bank. These are the only two sources of Capital. Debt and equity. Capital, of course, forms the foundation for what the business will be able to do, how much equipment it can have, how much inventory, how much of the capital its customers can use in the time it takes to collect the money due from sales, and so on. And, as a starting point of measurement, it also puts a limit on what the amount of Sales is likely to be."

"Exactly how does that work?" I asked.

"Well," he replied, "let's assume we are going into the business of assembling a line of small mechanical products and that we have raised a total of one million dollars in initial capital from a group who will be the owners of the business. We will find from looking at similar types of companies that we can expect to do no more than about three million dollars in Sales with our one million of Capital...that for our kind of business, one dollar of Capital will support about three dollars of Sales."

I was somewhat confused. "You say that would be the figure for *our* kind of business...the assembly of a line of small mechanical products. Does that mean there is a different number for every other kind of business?"

The Millionaire Manager nodded. "Yes, it does. And the measurement used to show this is called *turnover*. It works this way. If we have Sales of $3.0 million divided by our Capital of $1.0 million, we have a turnover of 3.0, meaning we are turning our Capital three times a year. And if we have two parts of the equation, we can always find the third," he explained as he walked to his whiteboard and wrote...

$$\frac{Sales}{Capital} = Turnover$$

So ...

Turnover x Capital = Sales Potential

"In this case," he concluded, "we know how much Capital we have, and we also know what the average turnover is for the kind of business we plan to operate. So by multiplying the two together, we very quickly get a picture of the Dollar Volume of Sales we can expect to support for the year."

"I see. But you said there were different figures for different types of business," I persisted. "Are they a lot different?"

"Quite different. The turnover rates will range from less than one in heavy industries such as steel, petroleum, and cement — to an average of ten times a year for supermarket operations where most of the capital is tied up in inventory. If the inventory is not turning rapidly in a supermarket, of course, you're not going to stay in business very long."

"So *Capital is your beginning point* as a five percent manager. I see how it works to determine the Dollar Volume of Sales it will support, but how do you control the Capital itself? You said it was used to supply the business with Equipment and Inventory and so forth. How can you make sure it isn't all tied up in one place...in Inventory, for example...so that you don't have enough cash on hand to pay the bills or meet the payroll?"

I could see that he liked my question because he went immediately to the whiteboard, anxious to explain his next point.

And this time, I smiled as I watched him write...

Millionaire Manager

A
Five Percent Manager
limits the
management of Capital
to five percent
of all the detail
found on the
Balance Sheet.

"By doing this," he explained, tapping his finger on the board, "I am concerned only with how the Capital is used, not where it came from. This can be measured and controlled in just five groups," he added, writing again on his whiteboard…

Controlling Capital

Cash

Receivables

Inventory

Equipment

(Payables)

Total Capital

"What do Payables mean, and what do they have to do with the use of Capital?" I asked, as I felt he was getting ahead of me.

"Think of it this way," he said. "Capital in business is used to supply what we call *assets*, things like inventory and equipment and so on. But there is another source that also supplies assets for a short term, and that is the various companies from which we buy inventory, supplies, and equipment. As you know, we very seldom pay cash on delivery since these suppliers will usually give us terms of about thirty days to pay our bills. The *Payables* then account for the assets used in the business that are supplied from this source."

"Then the total assets in a business must be larger than the total Capital," I interjected.

"Exactly!" he replied. "Assets are larger than Capital by the amount supplied by the Payables."

"That's fine, but I still don't see how you manage these five groups. How can you decide how much should be in each one?" I persisted.

The Millionaire Manager had already anticipated my question and was once again at the whiteboard. "I manage each of these five groups with the same tool I have already described to you...the average turnover of investment expected for this type of business," he said.

"You mean that there is also a series of these turnover numbers that in turn apply to the five groups that measure the use of Capital?" I asked, wondering where he got all of this material.

"Yes, there is," he replied, "and they are available in several different financial publications, although anyone can develop them simply by studying the reports of other companies engaged in the same line of business."

"What are the five individual turnover rates for the type of business we are talking about...that of assembling a line of mechanical products?"

"Here is how the total would break down," he explained, as he wrote the following on the whiteboard...

	Turnover
Cash	40.0
Receivables	8.0
Inventory	7.0
Plant & Equipment	5.5
Payables	(7.1)
Capital	3.0

"But how does that tie into the total of 3.0 for the total Capital?" I demanded. "It looks as though it would add up to much more."

The Millionaire Manager nodded. "Yes, it does appear that way when only the turnover rates are given, but if we try it another way, maybe it will be more understandable."

And this time he wrote…

Sales Divided by Turnover = Amount

Cash	$3,000,000	40.0	$75,000
Receivables	3,000,000	8.0	375,000
Inventory	3,000,000	7.0	428,500
Equipment	3,000,000	5.5	545,500
Total Assets	3,000,000	2.1	1,424,000
Payables	3,000,000	(7.1)	(424,000)
Capital	$3,000,000	3.0	$1,000,000

"You see," he continued, "since each of the five groups represents only a *part* of the total Capital measured against the total Sales, it is the same as saying that each of the five should amount to a certain Percent of the Sales. If we try it once more that way, I think you will see what I'm driving at. For example," he continued, "a turnover of 40.0 for Cash is the same as saying Cash should be one-fortieth of Sales, or 2.5%. In the same manner, Inventory with a turnover of 7.0 should be one-seventh of Sales, or 14.3% and so on. Putting them all together...it will look like this..."

	Turnover	Percent to Sales
Cash	40.0	2.5%
Receivables	8.0	12.5%
Inventory	7.0	14.3%
Equipment	5.5	18.1%
Total Assets	2.1	47.4%
Payables	(7.1)	(14.1%)
Capital	3.0	33.3%

"Yes, I can see now how it all comes together. But if it is simply a matter of dividing up the total Capital as a Percent of Sales, why not do it that way in the first place?" I asked. "Why bother to go through the calculation of turnover rates at all?"

The Millionaire Manager smiled at my question. "That's a very reasonable point," he agreed, "if we were only going to use the measurement just once in our management of the Balance Sheet. But you see, we are going to use it a second time in our five percent management of the Income Statement where the percentages wouldn't work."

"But," I countered, "we have already made that connection, the fact that the turnover will limit the level of sales income that the Capital can support. For the business we were discussing, you said that a turnover of 3.0 would apply. Where else does the turnover rate have anything to do with the Income Statement?"

"With the *Profit required* as a percent of the sales dollar," he replied, leaving it at that and waiting for my reaction.

"The Profit *required*?" I asked, thinking that I had misunderstood him.

"Yes, required," he answered. "I have a different approach to Profit than the ninety-five percent managers had. But we will come to that later. Right now, I want to show you how the turnover rate interacts with the profit rate on the sales dollar. You are familiar with the meaning of *Return on Investment*?"

"Yes, in a general sort of way," I replied, not sure where all this was heading.

"Well, for the moment, let's assume we want to earn a certain rate of return on our Capital...say 10.0%...just to pick a number by way of example. We haven't decided yet what kind of a business we want to go into, so we will need to know what the profit rate on Sales will have to be in several types of businesses in order to produce the 10.0% Return on Capital."

"And that will depend on what the turnover rate can be?" I responded, sensing that this was what he was leading up to.

"Exactly!" the Millionaire Manager replied. "And using our arbitrary 10.0% Return on Capital as an example, here is how the two come together," he added as he drew up the following on his whiteboard...

Type of Business	Turnover	x	Profit Rate	=	Return
Heavy Industry	1.0		10.0%		10.0%
Light Manufacturing	2.0		5.0%		10.0%
Assembly	3.0		3.3%		10.0%
Merchandising	4.0		2.5%		10.0%
/	/		/		/
Supermarkets	10.0		1.0%		10.0%

"So you see," he continued, "the higher the turnover rate, the lower the requirement for the percent return on every dollar of Sales. We will talk a bit later about what the rate of return on Capital ought to be, but for now do you see how turnover affects Profit?"

"As long as we are attempting to meet a certain objective rate of return on Capital, I do…" I conceded, "but I still don't see how you can pick a definite rate as a requirement for Profit. I thought Profit was what was left over after you subtracted all of the costs and expenses from the Income."

"That is the traditional definition of Profit," he agreed. "Wait a bit and I'll give you a better one. Right now, let's see if you understand my five percent management of the Balance Sheet and why I start with that report rather than with the Income Statement. Let's put down a few of the major points," he added, returning to the whiteboard.

Capital

- Comes from ownership money and/or borrowed money.

- Is the foundation of the business.

- Divided into Sales equals turnover.

- Turnover depends on the nature of the business.

- Turnover will limit the attainable Sales volume.

- Turnover determines the Rate of Return required on Sales.

I thought over these major points he was describing and went back in my mind to all of the various steps we had discussed. Some had been rather familiar, but there were many others that I had found new and rather perplexing. I felt I needed more time to get a solid grasp of what the Millionaire Manager was telling me and suggested we stop for a while.

"Yes, I believe you have had enough for one day," he agreed. "I see you have made quite a few notes on what we have covered so far. Why not take a break now to think it over and see what questions you may have. Let's see...this is Tuesday. Take a day to think it over and I will see you again on Thursday morning."

I was grateful for the suggestion and thanked him for his time. As I folded my notebook and left his office, my mind was already jumping ahead to questions I would bring back to him.

I was back in his office early on Thursday morning and found the Millionaire Manager ready and waiting for me, his desk again noticeably bare of the usual clutter. He greeted me with a smile that I had begun to associate with his relaxed attitude in business.

"Now that you've had some time to think over our discussion on Tuesday, what questions do you have about my *five percent management* of the Balance Sheet?" he asked.

"I have several, and I think it might help if I took them in the order in which you listed the management of the five parts of that report. First, with Cash, which you say you manage on a 40.0 times turn, or 2.5% of Sales. Does this mean managing the *cash flow* of the business, a term I have heard a lot about?"

"If the measurement is used not only on the past results to date but on a projection or forecast of results for the near future, it does," he replied. "It will assure me that I have sufficient cash to meet the operating needs of the business."

"I thought it might work that way," I agreed, "but I have no idea how the next point ties in. You say the Receivables due from your customers should have a turnover of 8.0 for an average balance of Capital tied up in this asset account equivalent to 12.5% of Sales. What does this have to do with the collection of the money — whether your customers are paying on time or not?"

"There is a direct connection between the two," the Millionaire Manager asserted, as he started again for his favorite teaching tool, the whiteboard. "The turnover rate first of all determines the Percent of Sales that is tied up in the Receivables asset," he pointed out, "but if we divide the turnover rate into the number of days in the year, we will find the average number of days Sales outstanding, that is, how many days it is taking to collect the average account. And to simplify the measurement, we use the banker's year of 360 days," he added, as he wrote the following:

Collection of Receivables

$$\frac{\text{Number of Days in Year}}{\text{Turnover Rate}} = \text{Number of Days in Collection}$$

$$\frac{360}{8.0} = 45 \text{ Days Average Collection}$$

"But I thought your terms of sale were 30 days net," I objected. "Why do you plan on 45 days, tying up that much of your capital an extra 15 days?"

"For many reasons," he answered quickly. "There may be questions on the customer's part concerning the shipment that may call for an adjustment in the billing. The billing itself or the payment may be delayed in the mail, and then there will always be some customers who are always late as well as a few who never pay. I find the 45 days acceptable on average, and besides *I plan on enough profit to pay for the use of the capital*, as we will see a bit later."

I did a bit of mental arithmetic and asked, "So if every one of your accounts paid exactly on time in 30 days...the turnover of Receivables would be 12.0 times a year?"

"Your calculation is quite right," he agreed, "but that isn't about to happen in my line of business," he added with a laugh.

"My next question has to do with the turnover of Inventory — not with the rate itself, but with the method you used. You divided the average inventory investment into the sales dollars, as I recall. Isn't that wrong? Shouldn't you have divided it into the Cost of Goods Sold rather than the Sales?"

"I understand your confusion," he said. "What you are referring to is the operating measurement of *physical* turnover, how many days supply of inventory I have on hand. That is a useful measurement for the inventory manager in planning his stocking requirements, but it is not a financial control or measurement. In measuring turnover related to Sales, I am measuring the *turnover of money* tied up in the inventory asset account, not the physical turnover of the number of pieces in stock."

"Then there are two meanings to the term *turnover* when you speak of Inventory?"

"Yes," the Millionaire Manager agreed, "but I find the financial turnover the more important of the two."

My questions and challenges were being answered or rebuffed rather efficiently, and I wondered how long it would take him to dispose of my last one. I had no problem with the use of turnover related to the investment in Plant and Equipment; that seemed to be quite straightforward. I was, however, totally confused with his turnover measurement of the Payables.

"One last question, then. For the Payables group you show a turnover rate in parentheses...I guess as a negative...and I can't understand what it means. Why do you do it, and how does it work?"

"I'll admit that one is a bit confusing," he agreed. "Let's see if this will help. First of all, the turnover is shown in parentheses because we are dealing with a *liability*...with money owed to our suppliers...not with an asset. With the assets, we would want the turnover to increase up to some reasonable limit since that would indicate improved efficiency in the use of Capital...more Sales for every dollar of Capital employed. For the Payables, it is just the reverse," he explained. "Let me show you what I mean," he added as he began to write on the whiteboard...

Turnover of Payables

$$\frac{\text{Sales } \$3,000,000}{\text{Turnover } (7.1)} = \$424,000 \text{ Payables}$$

Payables are supporting $424,000 in Assets

$$\frac{\text{Sales } \$3,000,000}{\text{Turnover } (6.0)} = \$500,000 \text{ Payables}$$

Payables are supporting $500,000 in Assets

The Millionaire Manager turned from the whiteboard and asked, "Do you see what I meant by a reverse direction for the Payables? What we want here is not a higher turnover, as in the case of the asset groups, but a *lower turnover*, again, within reason...a point we will cover later on."

"Yes, I see now," I agreed, as I followed his explanation. "*A lower turnover of the Payables means more assets are being furnished by our suppliers so that the need for more of our own Capital is reduced.* That sounds like good financial management."

"I'm glad you see the point," he smiled. "Not many managers even see the management of Payables as any part of profit management in the first place, just as an operating need to meet the due dates. Payables can be managed through negotiating terms, seeking out alternate suppliers, getting goods on consignment, and so on. It is simply part of the management of Capital," he concluded.

At this point, he left the whiteboard and returned to his seat. "I think we have covered all of the major points I wanted to give you with respect to the management of the Balance Sheet," he mused. "Do you have any final questions about my plan of *five percent management* of this report?"

"Let me summarize," I replied. "The Balance Sheet lists a hundred or more items in considerable detail, details of the several individual asset groups as well as further details of the liability accounts, the monies you owe to your suppliers or to the banks. In addition, there is more detail shown in the capital section...where the capital came from and who it belongs to...the owners or the bank. If I understand you correctly, you manage only about five percent of all this knowing that if you can control the totals, you won't need to worry about the pieces. Have I got that right?"

"Couldn't have done better myself," he said with a grin. "Let's move on to the other side of the picture. We have a lot of ground to cover on the Income Statement."

"The Income Statement," he continued, "can usually have more detail than the Balance Sheet, depending on the number of functions and departments in the business. That makes it even more important to use my *five percent rule* here," he observed. "If I don't, I could quickly lose control of the operating results," he added.

"Well, the Balance Sheet certainly broke down rather nicely into your five groups, but there would seem to be more than five you would need on this report. What are your five points on the Income Statement, and how do you decide which ones are important?" I asked.

"Back to the whiteboard," he said with a smile. "There are only five items that matter. Let me show you what they are."

He erased the board and began to write...

Five Percent Management of the Income Statement

- *Dollar Volume of Sales*
- *Variable Costs*
- *Gross Margin*
- *Period Expenses*
- *Operating Profit*

"Five points again!" I commented. "Okay. Let's start with the Dollar Volume of Sales. Don't we already have that from our management of the Balance Sheet...the $3.0 million we developed as the 3.0 times turnover of the $1.0 million of Capital?"

"We have that figure as the probable Sales dollars *attainable* with that much Capital," he replied, "but now we have to check some other controlling factors such as our expected share of the market, our production capability, our marketing plan, and our selling expense budget, to mention just a few. To make it simple, let's assume that all of these factors do add up to a Sales budget of $3.0 million for the year. That assumes a lot of work in this area has been done, but it gets us quickly past point number one and on to the next, which I think will require much more in the way of an explanation," he warned.

"I'm sure that has to do with what you listed as Variable Costs," I noted. "I have a vague idea of what this probably means, but could you be more specific?"

"Yes, I think I can," the Millionaire Manager replied. "It has to do with the *behavior of costs and expenses*, how they will react under changing conditions of Production and Sales. When you approach it this way, you will find that there are only two basic groups in any business, one of which will change almost directly in proportion to a change in the dollar volume of output, and the other which is indifferent to a change in volume in the short term and changes only in steps over a period of time. Do you begin to see the meaning behind these terms?" he asked.

"Let's stay with the Variable Costs for the moment," I said. "Can you give me an example of what they would include?"

"Certainly!" he replied. "There are only a few in most companies. They would include, first of all, the cost of materials used in production or purchased for resale. They may also include the labor costs of production although this is changing rapidly with automation and a trend in the policies of many companies to maintain steady employment rather than let the labor force go up and down with changes in the level of Production and Sales," he added.

"Aren't there also some variable costs of Sales as well as variable costs of Production?" I asked.

"There are, and I was coming to them. The group of items making up the difference between *Gross Sales* and *Net Sales* is one area of Variable Costs. These would generally include Discounts, Returns & Allowances, Warranty Expenses, and the like. Further down on the statement, we would also find Commissions, Royalties, and Freight Out...all of which typically will vary in almost direct proportion to the Dollar Volume of Sales."

"You have segregated these costs and expenses into one of your *five points of management*," I mused, "but how do you control this group?"

"The Variable Costs & Expenses are measured and controlled either as unit costs in the area of Production or as a Percent to Sales for the variable selling costs. The dollar amounts have no significance until they are related to the dollars of Sales. Perhaps this diagram will help to illustrate what I mean," he suggested, writing again on the whiteboard...

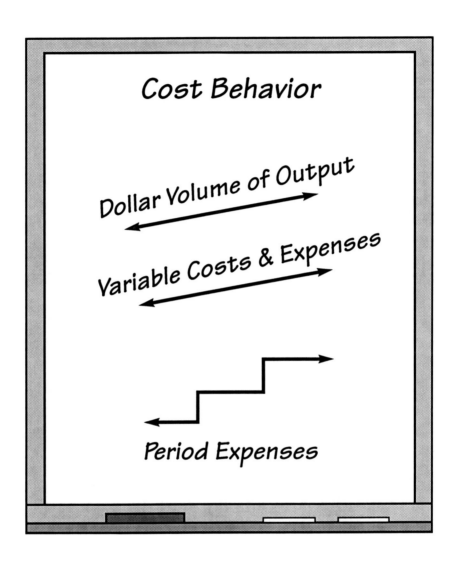

"So the Variable Costs & Expenses are *volume oriented,* whereas Period Expenses get that name from the fact that they are *time oriented* — that they respond to change only over a period of time. Is that what you mean by these terms?"

"Exactly! And since we're on the subject, we might as well go directly to the third point of my *five percent management* of the Income Statement while we're at it...the Period Expenses group. We can come back to the question of Gross Margin afterwards," he added. "Period Expenses will include such items as depreciation, rent, local taxes, salaries, travel, and utilities — items that do not change in direct proportion to a change in volume in the short term but change gradually over a period of time in response to new levels of output, either higher or lower."

"Aren't these expenses also generally measured and controlled as a percent of something?" I asked, thinking of an article I had read about the use of overhead rates.

"They are, but they shouldn't be," he declared rather emphatically. "When you mix the Period and Variable Costs & Expenses together and try to manage and control them in the same way, it's like putting apples and oranges into one pot. They are not alike, and they need to be measured and controlled separately. Variable Costs are expected to change with a change in volume. Period Expenses are not, except over a span of time, as new levels of output are reached."

"What would happen if you tried to manage or control the Period Expenses as a Percent of Sales? Wouldn't that keep them in line?" I asked, thinking he might be missing a point.

"On the contrary," he pointed out, "if I managed salaries as a Percent of Sales, for example, and Sales went up...say 15% over plan...I would then make an allowance of 15% for an increase in salary expense when, in fact, no increase at all would be justified. The higher budget allowance could then cover up a possible actual increase of say 5% or so which should not have taken place. The expense would be out of control and I wouldn't know it."

"I think I see your point," I said. "Let's go back to the second item...the one you listed as Gross Margin."

"All right," smiled the Millionaire Manager, "but first make a note of this..."

And he wrote on the whiteboard...

Period Expenses

are controlled in

Dollar Amounts Planned

versus

Dollar Amounts Incurred

He came back to his desk and sat down. "Now, let's define what we are talking about. The term *Gross Margin* simply refers to the difference between Sales and Variable Costs — how much is left after the Variable Costs are subtracted from the Sales."

"Simple enough. But how do you control the Gross Margin as one of your five steps of management of the Income Statement?" I asked.

"It's very simple," the Millionaire Manager responded, no doubt thinking that I should have known any control of his would be a simple one. "I control it through the Gross Margin Percent to Sales...a point of measurement that I establish ahead of time."

"You mean you set a standard or target ahead of time for what the Gross Margin Percent to Sales ought to be?" I thought I must have missed a point here, since we hadn't discussed what the Variable Costs ought to be in the first place.

"Yes, I do it by estimating the amount of *value added* to the product I am offering for sale. There is a whole range here from a low of about 10.0% Gross Margin for the supermarket — where the value added is simply one of distribution, the convenience provided to the customer of bringing a few thousand items together for sale in one place...all the way to a 70.0% Gross Margin, or higher, for the computer manufacturing company that adds a value in technology that the customer cannot do for himself."

"And where does our business fit in," I asked, "the assembly of mechanical products we were using as an example?"

"It should have about a 40.0% Gross Margin...a figure a bit over the halfway point from low to high...since assembly contains more value added than just distribution but certainly less than high technology," he explained.

"But suppose your Variable Costs turn out to be greater than the other 60.0%. How can you control one without knowing the other?" I questioned, thinking that I had perhaps missed a point somewhere along the line.

"This way," he smiled, turning again to the whiteboard. "I simply back into the amount *allowed*," he added, as he wrote the following...

"You see," he went on, "I manage the Variable Costs & Expenses as the amount allowed to give me the 40.0% margin I had set as a standard for my business."

"How can you make that work?" I wondered.

"By setting limits at the operating level for the several elements that make up the total of the Variable Costs," he explained. "For example, this is how I think they should break down for that assembly business," he went on, adding some more figures to the whiteboard...

Variable Costs & Expenses Allowed

Item	Percent of Sales
Product Cost	40.0%
Sales Commissions	10.0%
Discounts & Allowances	5.0%
Freight Out	5.0%
Total	60.0%

"My managers can then manage the pieces in any reasonable manner that will hold the total of the Variable Costs at 60.0%. They can change the Commission rate for the salespeople, the sales terms governing Discounts, Allowances, and Freight, for example, to accommodate a change in the product cost as necessary. I do not manage the detail," the Millionaire Manager continued. "I am only concerned with the results."

"Let's see, we have now covered the first three of your five points of control for the Income Statement...the Sales, the Variable Costs, and the Gross Margin. Is your next step to estimate the Period Expenses required for the business and then subtract them from the Gross Margin to arrive at the operating profit?" I asked, thinking this must be the logical sequence.

"No. In fact, we are going to back into the Period Expenses *allowed* for the business, much as we did in arriving at the Variable Costs. We're going to back into it by first determining the Profit *required*," he added with a smile.

"But I thought we covered that," I protested, "when we talked about the profit rate on Sales required to meet various rates of turnover."

"We did, but now we have to update our example to meet today's need in the marketplace. You remember we picked an arbitrary 10.0% rate of return on Capital just by way of example when we discussed the relationship between Turnover and the profit rate on Sales. But we don't know yet if this return is adequate given the type of business and level of risk we're assuming," he added. "We will need to test this assumption."

"How are we going to do that?" I asked, wondering where this new step was going to lead us.

"By starting with a new definition of Profit," he stated. "As I recall our earlier conversation, you referred to Profit as *the amount left over* after all costs and expenses were subtracted from Income."

"Yes, I did. Isn't that the usual way of defining it?"

"It is," he acknowledged, "but it amounts to just a bookkeeping definition, not an economic one. What we need is an approach to profit that will define it in terms of economic *need*, not a bookkeeping balance," and he wrote the following on his whiteboard...

PROFIT

is the

Compensation Accruing

to the Entrepreneur

for the

Assumption of Risk.

"In simple terms," he went on, "Profit is a cost of doing business. It is just as real as the cost of materials or the cost of labor or rent or supplies, even though it is considered an *imputed cost* rather than a recorded one. But then," he added, "so is the charge for depreciation of Equipment, so we shouldn't have any trouble dealing with the concept."

"But if the Profit is a cost of doing business, someone has to say what that cost is. Who does that and how do they know?" I demanded, feeling very confused over this whole conversation.

"The marketplace decides what the cost is," he explained. "It's simply our job to interpret that decision and then apply it to our business. Let's start with another figure from the marketplace, and let's assume you are going to invest that one million dollars of Capital we had in securities of the U.S. government, probably the lowest risk investment in the world. What rate of return would you get in today's market?"

"About 5.0% to 6.0%," I answered, thinking of the yield available on long-term government bonds.

"And if you could get that much on the lowest risk available," he asked, "what rate of return would you want if you put the million dollars of capital into our assembly business instead?"

"A lot higher!" I acknowledged, seeing his point immediately.

"Of course! Here is the picture we are talking about," he said, as he drew the following diagram...

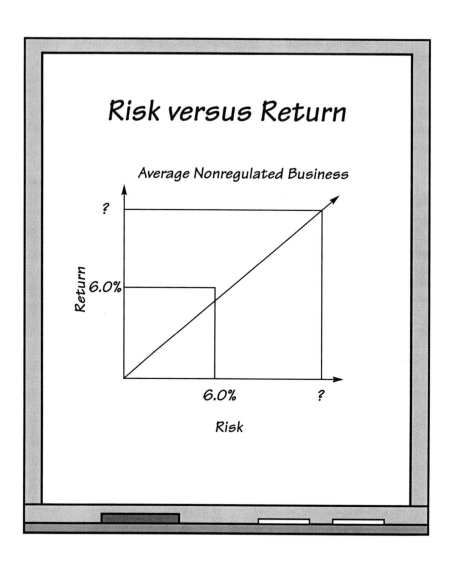

"Okay, I get the picture," I said. "The rate of return should be much higher for what is obviously a much higher risk. But how do you put a number on it?"

The Millionaire Manager was ready for the question.

"We don't," he replied. "As I said...the marketplace will do it for us. There seem to be two rules of thumb that are used. One is a multiple of interest rates such as the prime rate for money, and the other is a multiple of the yield available on government bonds. The latter is a bit simpler," he continued, "because you just approximately double the government bond yield to get the *cost of capital* rate, the rate of return on Capital required for the average business."

"That would put our *Profit requirement* at 12.0%?" I asked.

"It would," he replied. "But remember, we are dealing with an approximate order of magnitude, not with accounting precision. However, approximations of this sort are already present in the accounting process, as in charges for depreciation, so we are not breaking any new ground in determining the cost of capital employed."

"So you have a *Profit requirement* of 12.0% on the $1.0 million of capital in our assembly business. That comes to $120,000. Is that before or after income taxes?"

"That has to be *after* tax for the business, which of course becomes *before* tax for the investor...just as the interest on government bonds would be a before-tax return. To cover state and federal income tax provisions of about 40.0%, we will have to divide that figure by 60.0% to a pretax cost of Capital or *Profit requirement* of a 20.0% Return on Capital," he concluded.

"That seems like an awfully high figure," I observed, thinking of the typical net profit margins of 5.0% I was used to seeing.

"It is high. But so are the costs of debt and inflation," he pointed out. "It's not a question of choice; it's a matter of survival," he added quickly.

"But can a business achieve that kind of profit rate on its Capital?" I persisted.

"It can if its managers will all become *five percent managers*," he answered with a smile.

"Now that you have the Profit required...a pretax 20.0% return on the $1.0 million of Capital, a total of $200,000...you said the next step was to back into the Period Expenses allowed."

"Yes. Here is how it would work," he agreed, writing...

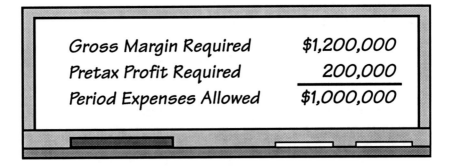

"So the Period Expenses group is actually the last of your five points of management of the Income Statement," I joined in.

"It is in my system," the Millionaire Manager replied, rather emphatically. "The ninety-five percent managers all seemed to put it first and then wondered why the profits weren't there," he added. "I guess they were just too busy to plan."

I thought about all of the various expenses that made up the overhead of a typical business, the items he referred to as Period Expenses, and wondered how he could decide how much of the total *allowed* should be spent on each of the expenses. I asked him about it.

"My first step," he explained, "is to separate the total into two groups, the *Committed* Expenses and the *Discretionary* Expenses. The first group, the Committed Expenses, will be those that are more or less locked in for the short term once I have set them in motion. The Discretionary Expenses are those that I will be able to change more frequently as the need arises."

"Can you give me an example of the Committed Expenses?"

"Certainly," he replied, turning again to his whiteboard where he wrote...

Committed Period Expenses

- Depreciation
- Rent
- Property Taxes
- Insurance
- Heat
- Light
- Water

"These pretty much represent the cost of simply being in business," he went on, "as opposed to the cost of operations, the more discretionary costs of Production, Sales, and Administration."

"But what about interest expense? Isn't that a Committed Expense?" I asked, thinking of the requirement to pay the bank for amounts borrowed.

"That's how many managers view it," he agreed. "But remember, in our determination of Profit, we are concerned only with the *use* of Capital in the business, not with its source. Interest represents the cost of debt capital. Including interest as a period cost would result in a double charge for the use of debt — once in the inclusion of debt capital in the investment base and a second time in the reduction of earnings for the interest expense on the same debt capital."

"Okay, going back to the Period Expenses, how do you decide the amount that should be set aside for the first group, the Committed Expenses?" I persisted.

"By knowing the approximate amount the second group will probably require. The Discretionary portion of the Period Expenses will be largely *people oriented*, and I have found, from experience, that this group will account for about two-thirds of the so-called overhead in the average business. Knowing that need, I can have only the other one-third of the total for the Committed Expenses," he pointed out.

The Millionaire Manager then went on to explain how this approach to the amount allowed for these expenses would, in turn, dictate the size and choice of location of buildings, decisions as to the level of investment in equipment, and so on.

"It is a disciplined approach," he said, "one the ninety-five percent managers didn't bother with."

"The total amount allowed for Period Expenses thus breaks down this way," he continued, as he added the following figures to his notes on the whiteboard.

Total Period Expenses Allowed	$1,000,000
One-Third Committed Expenses	300,000
Two-Thirds Discretionary Expenses	$700,000

"That looks like a top-down approach to planning," I commented. "But don't you have to then get involved in the question of how much will be spent for each element of the Discretionary Expenses?"

"No. I simply start with a plan for my organization, an outline of the various functions required for the business, a step which will determine the cost of salaries and benefits. The remaining expenses will then be determined in detail by the managers responsible, but always within the limits allowed. I let them handle the details. I stay with my *five percent rule*," he concluded.

I digested this bit of his philosophy as I reviewed my notes on his management of the Income Statement. He seemed to have covered all of the salient points, but I wanted to get an overall picture and felt that perhaps it was my turn at the whiteboard. "Is this how an Income Statement looks with your five points of control?" I asked, writing the numbers from my notes.

Income Statement

Sales	$3,000,000
Variable Costs	1,800,000
Gross Margin @ 40.0%	1,200,000
Period Expenses	1,000,000
Operating Profit	200,000
Percent to Sales	6.7%
Capital Employed	1,000,000
Turnover	3.0
Pretax Return on Capital	20.0%

"Yes, I guess that's how it would look if I got that kind of report. But I never receive copies of the Income Statement," he added surprisingly, "nor do I receive a copy of the Balance Sheet. We have them, of course, for the auditors and the tax collector, and I do find them useful as files if I have to look something up once in a while," he added with a smile.

"Files?" I said, unbelievingly.

"Exactly. As I pointed out earlier, those reports can run to a hundred pieces of detail. I'm not interested in details, just results. I pay other people to look after the details. Why should I do their jobs for them?"

"But you must have some kind of financial report just to keep track of your five points of management. If you don't get either the Income Statement or the Balance Sheet...what do you get?"

This last question was apparently the one he had been waiting for. With a rather self-satisfied grin, he went to his desk and took out a single sheet of paper.

"This is the only report I get once a month," he said. "I call it my *Five Percent Control Report*," he added. "And since I cannot control the income tax rates, I have put all my measurements on a pretax basis." He handed me the paper...

The Millionaire Manager's Five Percent Control Report

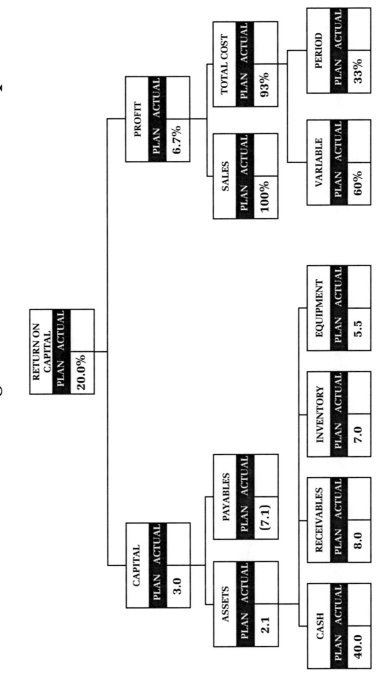

Millionaire Manager 73

"The left-hand side of this model," he explained, "contains the five points of control that I need from the Balance Sheet, each of them measured in terms of the Turnover Rate on Sales. The right-hand side contains the five points of control I need from the Income Statement, each of them measured as a Percent of Sales. This model actually brings these two financial statements...the Balance Sheet and the Income Statement...together into one common report, one which shows the interaction of Capital and Profit — Profit and Capital."

I could see he was quite pleased with the new report he was showing me, but I felt I needed to know more.

"Are you saying that this takes the place of the usual financial statements?" I asked. "Aren't they important by themselves?"

"Not only are they NOT important by themselves," he replied emphatically, "one of the two without the other is not only totally meaningless, it can be dangerously misleading."

"Take a look at my Five Percent Control Report for the assembly business we were discussing," he continued. "Starting at the top, we see a plan to earn a 20.0% pretax Return on Capital by turning our Capital 3.0 times a year multiplied by a pretax Profit of 6.7% on every dollar of Sales. Do you see how the two interact to produce the required 20.0% Return on Capital?" he prodded.

"Yes, I do. Whatever happens to one will affect the needs of the other," I mused.

"Precisely. Now let's take these two reports separately and assume the Return on Sales increases to 6.8% from our plan of 6.7%. Many managers would see that as a modest gain in profitability *without realizing that the turnover of capital had, for example, fallen from 3.0 to only 2.9 times, a combination that was actually taking the profitability down* a notch from the 20.0% planned to a rate of only 19.7% on capital employed. Let me show you over here how that works," he added, returning to his whiteboard to write...

Millionaire Manager

Interaction of Profit & Capital

Turnover	x	Return on Sales	=	Return on Capital
3.0		6.7%		20.0%
2.9		6.8%		19.7%
2.8		6.9%		19.3%
2.7		7.0%		18.9%
2.6		7.1%		18.5%

"You see," he continued, "most managers use only the Income Statement as a measurement of business success, referring to the Balance Sheet as a separate document simply to check on cash balances, inventory levels, and various financial ratios which affect their ability to meet current obligations. They usually make no connection between the two reports and can go on thinking they are gaining in profitability when in fact they are slowly going downhill," he concluded and returned to his chair as I digested this last piece of information.

"Well," he continued, "that about covers the basic parts of how to be *a five percent manager.* Do you think you understand how it works?"

"In planning a business, as we have done, I can see how each of the five steps is planned for the Balance Sheet and again for the Income Statement. But I'm not sure how you make it work on an ongoing basis when things change as they always do in any business. How can you keep your five steps on each side in balance with each other over the course of a year or more?" I asked.

The Millionaire Manager had again anticipated my question as he stood and went immediately to his whiteboard. "When things change, as they inevitably do in business," he proceeded, "is when my five percent control works best. Let's take one of the most changeable of the asset groups — the Inventory — and see what would happen to our assembly business if it were run by one of the ninety-five percent managers. Remember, they were checking on all of the detail and trying to manage each piece as a separate one-at-a-time problem. So let's assume that our Inventory turnover decreased from a planned rate of 7.0 to a low of only 5.4 — a change which would amount to an increase of $127,000 on our Balance Sheet," he concluded as he wrote on the board...

The 95% Managers Results

	Old	New
Capital Employed	$1,000,000	$1,127,000
Pretax Profit	$200,000	$200,000
Return on Capital	20.0%	17.7%

"So you see," he continued, "the increase in Inventory would amount to an increase in the total assets of the business as well as an increase in the amount of total Capital employed. And even if the profit rate on Sales was on plan at 6.7%, the target would be missed where it mattered most, in the rate of return on Capital."

"Yes, I follow the calculations, but if the same increase in Inventory took place under your *five percent management plan*, how would you handle it differently?" I asked, failing to see how his approach could change any of the numbers.

"Simply by adjusting some of the other *five points of control*, either on the Balance Sheet or on the Income Statement," he replied with a smile. "By compensating for the increase in Inventory with reductions in other asset groups, with a negotiated increase in the amount of Payables outstanding, or, if necessary, with an increase in the amount of Profit as a rate of return on Sales. Whatever it takes," he continued seriously, "to maintain the rate of return on Capital required."

"In other words, something else will have to be cut back to pay for the increase in Inventory?" I interjected.

"Exactly!" he agreed. "This is the discipline that my *five percent control* supplies. I must do everything possible to maintain the goal for the *required* return on Capital. And here's how we might do it in the example we just used. My first step, of course, would be to get the Inventory investment back in line with the plan. But let's assume that such a move is not feasible in the short term and that I am forced to look elsewhere. I am going to rule out any change in the Equipment group as not being subject to any effective adjustment in the short term since I have already assured myself that we have no excess investment in that asset group. Nor would I want to take the easy solution of simply letting the Cash balance shrink to pay for the inventory."

"Well, that leaves only the Receivables and the Payables as possible targets for adjustment on the Balance Sheet," I noted.

"You're quite right!" the Millionaire Manager agreed. "Let's see what we might do with those two groups to offset the increase in Inventory without, however, creating an adverse impact on our Sales or Profit. The Receivables, for example, were planned at a turnover of 8.0, which amounted to an average collection period of 45 days, as you will recall," he added. "If we pushed too far on collections, we could begin to hurt sales, and eventually profits, but it might be reasonable to improve that collection to around 42 days with a little more follow-up on our part. That would bring the turnover up to an 8.5 rate for the year, thus reducing the Capital by $22,100," he concluded.

"The last place we can turn for adjustment on the Balance Sheet is in the Payables group, and here our goal is to reduce the turnover and thus *increase* the Payables," he pointed out.

"You could do that by simply not paying all of the bills on time," I observed.

The Millionaire Manager shook his head sharply at that comment. "No, not that way," he said emphatically. "We will try to increase the Payables by negotiating with our suppliers for better terms, by trying to get some inventory placed with us on consignment, or whatever. I do not believe in just borrowing from our suppliers by stretching over the long term," he added. "No, if we do it the right way, I would see the possibility of reducing the turnover of Payables from the plan of 7.1 to no more than 6.8 — a step which would increase the use of assets from that direction and thus reduce the need for our own Capital by $17,200."

"Will those two changes add up to enough to offset the higher inventory?" I asked.

"Perhaps not," he admitted. "Our next step is to figure out how many dollars reduction these two steps would amount to." And, at this point, he did some figuring on the whiteboard…

Compensating for Inventory Increase

Original Capital	$1,000,000
Increase in Inventory	127,000
Decrease in Receivables	(22,100)
Increase in Payables	(17,200)
New Capital	$1,087,700
New Turnover	2.7
Return on Sales	6.7%
New Return on Capital	18.1%

"No, it's not enough," he conceded. "Those two changes will bring it back up a bit, but the results will still be short of the goal. We'll have to find the rest of the gain on the right-hand side of our equation, on the Income Statement itself," he pointed out.

"Well, I can see how you figured the changes in the Receivables and Payables amounts, but how can you apply this kind of a measurement to the Income Statement?" I demanded. "That won't decrease the Capital."

"No, it won't," he agreed. "But it can be made to pay for supporting a greater amount of Capital. Let's see how much the profit will now have to go up to finish the job," he added, writing the answer quickly on the whiteboard…

The Final Step

$$\frac{\text{Return on Capital Required } 20.0\%}{\text{Turnover Available } 2.7} = \text{Return on Sales Required } 7.4\%$$

7.4% x $3,000,000 Sales = $222,000 Profit Required

6.7% x $3,000,000 Sales = $200,000 Profit Planned

0.7% of $3,000,000 Sales = $22,000 Profit Increase Required

"So as a final step in bringing the business back on plan, you will need an increase of $22,000 in operating profit for the year. That's less than 1.0% of Sales — it doesn't sound like much of a change," I argued, as though that much improvement should come quite easily.

"It may be less than 1.0% of Sales," the Millionaire Manager agreed, "but that's not where I can count on getting the added profit. That would be an easy assumption of simply hoping it would happen. I've got to make sure it will happen, and that means taking steps to reduce costs."

"Where will you turn to do that?" I asked, feeling properly rebuked for my quick assumption that added sales was a solution to the profit requirement. (That word *requirement* was beginning to stick in my mind.)

"There is only one place to go," he continued. "I can't cut the Variable Costs without jeopardizing the Gross Margin, and the Committed Period Expenses can only be adjusted over a much longer span of time. It will have to come out of the people-oriented expenses, the group we described as the Discretionary Period Expenses," he concluded.

As he reached this point, I began to appreciate his use of the term *Discretionary Expenses* for this portion of the overhead. They were truly the only area where expenses could be reduced with the least amount of damage in the short term.

"You will recall that we set aside two-thirds of the $1,000,000 in total Period Expenses for the Discretionary group," he continued, "which amounted to $700,000, and the $22,000 cost reduction to increase profits will amount to 3.1% of these expenses. This will not be easy to come by, but it must be done if we are to maintain the required rate of return on our Capital."

The Millionaire Manager then returned to his desk and began to make notes on another copy of his Five Percent Control Report. "I have entered all of the adjustments we have made to offset the higher Inventory investment and still hold the targeted return on Capital," he pointed out, "and to highlight the interaction of Capital and Profit, I have circled the changes that combine to keep the business on plan."

The Millionaire Manager's Five Percent Control Report

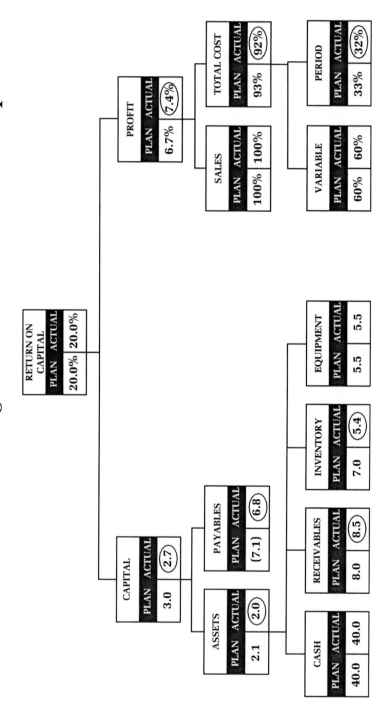

"You will notice," he said, pointing to his Five Percent Control Report, "how even a modest slippage in the turnover of Capital — from 3.0 to 2.7 — can cause a rather substantial reduction in costs on the operating side to offset it. The leverage is all on the use of the Capital side of the equation," he noted. "And a manager will find it much easier to manage his Capital properly in the first place rather than be forced into the difficult choices of where to effect cost reduction."

"I notice you didn't consider simply raising your selling prices as a solution to the higher profit required," I responded. "Wouldn't that be one other possibility?"

"Not really, not if I were already truly competitive in my pricing. I would be asking the customer to pay for inefficient management of my inventory or for unnecessary costs in my overhead structure. It sounds like an easy solution, but it will seldom work in practice," he admonished me.

"But do you actually make such adjustments in capital and operating expenses every month during the year?" I asked. "Do you really try to maintain that rigid a control over the return on Capital rate in the short term?"

"No, I do not. I made those adjustments simply as an example to demonstrate how the controls work to keep the business on target. If I acted blindly to every short-term change, I could end up limiting the very growth I hoped to achieve. Take that increase in Inventory that we just used as an example. If instead of merely being the result of poor asset management, let's assume it was done to meet a growing demand for the product, with a marked increase in the order backlog. Those orders would be shipped at a later date, and it might readily be shown that the higher inventory was at exactly the right level for *future sales*," he went on, "so that no corrective action need be taken."

"Do you have another five point control for measuring future results?" I asked, wondering if he perhaps did get involved in more detail than he had admitted to.

"No. No further steps nor any new tools," he replied with a smile. "I simply put more emphasis on the future than I do on the past, so that as we go through the year, I am measuring not only the actual results to date but a projection for the total year at all times, one which includes an up-to-date forecast for the remaining months of the year. And, at times, I may elect to modify this by using a twelve-month rolling projection, regardless of the timing of the business year," he added.

The Millionaire Manager went on to discuss the need to manage the business on an ongoing basis, looking ahead to what is about to happen and being willing to accept lower results in the short term as the price of winning in the longer term. This sparked a question that had been bothering me throughout the whole discussion.

"How do you decide how much you can sacrifice in the short-term results to pay for longer term profitability?" I wanted to know.

"That question has to be answered in a single word," he replied. "Judgment! There is no formula or report that I know of that will ever replace it," he continued. "My *five percent management controls* simply give me a much better chance of making the right judgment when the time comes."

I could see how the *five percent controls* would apply to manage the profitability of an overall business, but I wondered how they could be used to manage the profitability of a division or a particular product line. I asked him about it.

"My *five percent control techniques* can be applied to any divisional or product line analysis. You simply look to the actual assets managed in that division or product line, as well as the direct expenses actually incurred. To get a clear picture of the product line or divisional profitability, it is important to deal only with the direct capital employed and direct costs of the business. Generally accepted accounting practice will require the allocation of corporate overhead expenses to these divisions and/or product lines, and these costs need to be unraveled and removed from any analysis of Return on Invested Capital," he said.

"For instance, assume that your company has three divisions, with the following direct average assets for the year," he continued, as he turned to his whiteboard and wrote…

	Division A	Division B	Division C
Inventories	$60,000	$100,000	$40,000
Receivables	35,000	75,000	15,000
Equipment*	150,000	200,000	90,000
Less Payables	(20,000)	(45,000)	(10,000)
Net Capital Managed	$225,000	$330,000	$135,000

*Only equipment used exclusively in the operations of the particular division is included. Equipment and other fixed assets that are applicable across divisions are not allocated, as they are outside of the divisional manager's control.

"Assume further that you had the following operating results on the divisions from your accounting department."

	Division A	Division B	Division C	Total
Units Sold	50,000	30,000	20,000	100,000
Price ($)	8.00	15.00	7.50	10.00
Net Sales	$400,000	$450,000	$150,000	$1,000,000
Cost of Sales	330,000	270,000	100,000	700,000
Gross Profit	70,000	180,000	50,000	300,000
Percent to Sales	17.5%	40.0%	33.3%	30.0%
Selling Expenses	60,000	67,500	22,500	150,000
Administrative Exp.	47,000	39,000	14,000	100,000
Total Expenses	107,000	106,500	36,500	250,000
Pretax Profit	($37,000)	$73,500	$13,500	$50,000
Income Taxes				20,000
Net Earnings				$30,000

"Based on this, what conclusions would you draw?" he asked.

I looked at the numbers. "I would say that Division A is unprofitable, yielding only a 17.5% Gross Margin, which is not sufficient to cover its operating costs."

The Millionaire Manager smiled. "Yes, that would appear to be true, given the results under normal absorption accounting. But what if a closer examination of the expenses revealed that the Variable Cost of Goods Sold per unit for each division were as follows: Division A, $3.60; Division B, $6.00; and Division C, $2.00. Further, that Period Manufacturing Expenses, or fixed overhead, of $300,000 was allocated to all divisions based on the number of units produced and sold. In addition, the total selling expenses of $150,000 include $90,000 of general expenses that were allocated to each of the three divisions based on the net Dollar Volume of Sales, and the administrative expenses had been distributed as a Percent of the Cost of Sales. The only Direct Costs in selling expenses were as follows: Division A, $20,000; Division B, $30,000; and Division C, $10,000. If we redo the operating statement with the Fixed and Variable Costs properly identified and analyzed, we get a much different picture," he said, as he turned again to the whiteboard and wrote...

	Division A	Division B	Division C	Total
Units Sold	50,000	30,000	20,000	100,000
Price ($)	8.00	15.00	7.50	10.00
Net Sales	$400,000	$450,000	$150,000	$1,000,000
Direct Cost of Sales	180,000	180,000	40,000	400,000
Gross Margin	220,000	270,000	110,000	600,000
Price/Volume Ratio	55.0%	60.0%	73.0%	60.0%
Assignable Period Expense				
Selling Expense	20,000	30,000	10,000	60,000
Profit Contribution	$200,000	$240,000	$100,000	$540,000
Percent to Sales	50.0%	53.0%	67.0%	51.0%
Return on Capital Managed	89%	73%	74%	
Nonassignable Period Expense				
Manufacturing				300,000
Selling				90,000
Administrative				100,000
Total				$490,000
Pretax Profit				50,000
Income Taxes				20,000
Net Earnings				$30,000

The Millionaire Manager stepped away from his whiteboard. "You see, what emerges is that Division A is much more profitable than originally thought. The price volume, or P/V ratio, serves as a reliable measurement of the profit leverage inherent in higher volume for each division. Based on the P/V ratio, Division C now presents the greatest profit potential for growth, as opposed to Division B under the old analysis. In addition, this new analysis measures only those elements of fixed overhead, now identified as Assignable Period Expense, which exist solely in support of the operations of each division and therefore are under the divisional manager's control. The resulting measurement of Profit Contribution identifies the relative contribution of each division at this level of volume toward the recovery of corporate overhead and total operating profit. By measuring the Profit Contribution of each division, we have a guide as to how investment in each division might impact future profit potential."

I sat back and studied his numbers, wondering how many product lines I had abandoned in my own business over the years, thinking them unprofitable based on my old financial reports.

I had learned a great deal from the Millionaire Manager and was eager to get back and apply the five percent control methods to my own business. But I just needed to know one more thing.

"One final question. You keep referring to the profit in business as a requirement, as a cost of doing business. I followed your reasoning in arriving at the 20.0% pretax return on Capital employed, but is that high a return really necessary? What happens if you don't make it? Surely, you're still in business if the profit turns out to be a smaller one?" I pressed.

"Yes, as a matter of fact, I might still be in business for some time to come, and that very fact is one of the greatest obstacles in the path of good management. You see, by earning less than the required cost of capital rate, I would have begun a gradual liquidation of my Capital and called it Profit. This is exactly what the ninety-five percent managers did without realizing it."

He could see that I didn't quite follow his reasoning here, so he added, "I would be liquidating my Capital by not earning enough to replace it — by not earning enough to buy new equipment when the old had worn out, not enough to replace the inventory when it was used up — and, eventually, not enough to stay in business, particularly under increasing inflation."

"You mean you would run out of cash. Is that what you mean by liquidating your Capital?" I asked.

"Eventually, I would run out of cash," he agreed, "but in the short term, I would actually be increasing my Cash by liquidating my other assets and converting them into Cash. You see, the *cash flow usually increases as you start to go out of business*. This is what misled the ninety-five percent managers into thinking they were doing well," he concluded.

"In other words," I summed up, "*you are treating Profit as a measured requirement that must be met over a reasonable period of time, not just as a hoped-for target for the business?*"

The Millionaire Manager nodded enthusiastically. "Precisely! That's my method of putting a discipline into the financial plan for a business. After all, if all of my capital could be borrowed from the bank — in theory — I would certainly have an absolute requirement to pay for the use of that capital in the form of interest payments. Is there any reason to treat the capital borrowed from the owners any differently?"

That last point seemed to drive the lesson home. I had a new concept of profit in business...one far removed from the one I had grown accustomed to in reading most business reports. It was a tough discipline, but I could follow the reasoning. And then I asked one final question. "How many managers are actually managing their business this way?"

At this point, the Millionaire Manager leaned back in his chair and gave me a wide grin.

"Only about five percent," he replied, "and that's how they became millionaires."

The following pages contain pro forma statements and instructions to enable you to apply the techniques you have just learned to construct the Millionaire Manager's Five Percent Control Report for your own business.

Determine your company's profitability using the
Millionaire Manager ROIC Calculator™
available at:
www.MillionaireManager.com

Step Number One

Select copies of your two financial statements:
the Balance Sheet and the Income Statement
for a representative period of time.

Year-end statements would be preferable,
but if monthly or quarterly statements are used,
make certain that the figures for
Gross Sales & *Expenses* are *ANNUALIZED*
in calculating Turnover Rates.

> # *Step Number Two*

Extract from your own Balance Sheet
the amounts for each of the five control points
to conform to the example on the following page.

This will provide you with a direct measurement
of the Total Capital employed, a measurement not
shown on the accounting presentation.

In place of the ending balances,
the figures used should represent *Averages*
as being more representative of the amount
of Capital employed during the period
in which the profits were earned.

Average Capital Employed

	AMOUNT
CASH	_____
ACCOUNTS RECEIVABLE	_____
INVENTORY	_____
PLANT & EQUIPMENT	_____
TOTAL ASSETS	_____
PAYABLES	(_____)
INVESTED CAPITAL	_____

Step Number Three

Recast your Income Statement
to conform to the example on the following page.
In doing so, make note of these two items:

1. The Cost of Goods Sold
should include *Variable Costs only*.

The difference, if any,
can be shown below as
Manufacturing Period Expense.

2. Charges for interest on debt capital,
if incurred, should be omitted from the
statement for this purpose.

Properly treated, interest is not an
operating cost, but a *distribution of profit*.

The measurement of Return on Invested Capital
is thus before interest charges.

Income Statement Example

	AMOUNT
SALES	_____
VARIABLE COST OF GOODS SOLD	_____
GROSS MARGIN	_____
P/V RATIO	_____
PERIOD EXPENSES:	_____
MANUFACTURING	_____
SELLING	_____
ADMINISTRATIVE	_____
TOTAL PERIOD EXPENSES	_____
PRETAX OPERATING PROFIT	_____
AVERAGE CAPITAL EMPLOYED	_____
RETURN ON INVESTED CAPITAL	_____

Step Number Four

Determine the cost of capital, and thus the required Return on Invested Capital, based on the current yield on long-term U.S. government bonds as shown below:

U.S. Government Bonds Interest Rate	Pretax* Return Required
3.0%	10.0%
4.0%	13.3%
5.0%	16.7%
6.0%	20.0%
7.0%	23.3%
8.0%	26.7%
9.0%	30.0%
10.0%	33.3%
11.0%	36.7%
12.0%	40.0%
13.0%	43.3%
14.0%	46.7%
15.0%	50.0%
16.0%	53.3%
17.0%	56.7%
18.0%	60.0%
19.0%	63.3%
20.0%	66.7%

*Assumes a U.S. tax rate of 40.0%

> # *Step Number Five*

Complete the Millionaire Manager's Five Percent Control Report using the numbers you have computed in steps one through four.

Calculate your company's profitability using the
Millionaire Manager ROIC Calculator™
available at:
www.MillionaireManager.com

The Millionaire Manager's Five Percent Control Report

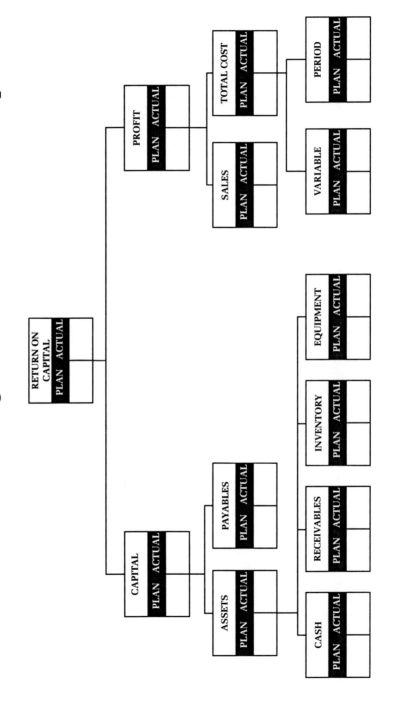

Millionaire Manager 113

When you have completed...

...the Control Report
for your own business,
you will have found the following:

1. The Return on Invested Capital
versus
the pretax required rate.

2. *The management of profitability is
the integrated management of
the Balance Sheet and the Income Statement.*

Thank you for reading this book.

For additional hands-on training and
easy transition in using these techniques,
we are pleased to offer you our
**Millionaire Manager
Profit Management Training Simplified
CDs and Online Courses.**

www.MillionaireManager.com

GLOSSARY

Accounts Receivable
Money owed by customers to businesses; amounts owed to business for goods and services sold by the business but not yet collected.

Accounts Payable
Money owed to vendors and suppliers for goods and services purchased on terms (e.g., 30 days).

Accumulated Earnings
The cumulative earnings of the business over time that have not been paid out to the shareholders as dividends.

Annualized
A statistical technique whereby figures for a period of less than a full year are extended to cover a 12-month period. For example, if sales for one month are $10,000, then annualized sales are $120,000 ($10,000 x 12 months).

Assets
The accumulation of total amounts owned by the business. Includes items such as cash, accounts receivable, inventory, plant and equipment, and so on.

Balance Sheet
Part of the financial statement that lists all the things you own: cash, inventory, equipment, and so on, as well as all of the amounts you owe to your suppliers or to the bank. It also shows how much capital you have put into the business and where it comes from.

Capital
The amount of money that someone has put up to get the business started and to allow it to continue and grow. In the beginning, it is usually all supplied by the owners and is called equity capital. Later, as time goes on, debt capital will probably be added as the business grows.

Cash Flow
The net of cash collected by the business minus cash paid out by the business during the year.

Committed Expenses
Expenses that are locked in for the short term and cannot be adjusted quickly. Examples include: depreciation, rent, property taxes, insurance, heat, light, water. Typically account for about one-third of total period expenses.

Cost of Capital
The required return on the capital invested in the business. Can be estimated by doubling the current yield on the long-term government bond, and dividing the result by 100% minus the effective tax rate of the business.

Cost of Goods Sold
The total costs incurred by the business in producing or acquiring product for resale.

Days Sales Outstanding
Represents the number of days it takes to collect sales revenue from customers. Calculated by dividing 360 days by the average turnover rate for accounts receivable.

Debt
Total amounts borrowed by the business. Includes bank loans, shareholder loans, employee loans, and equipment leases.

Depreciation
The recovery of the cost of equipment and property to the income statement over the estimated useful life of such asset.

Direct Costs
Costs that are directly related to or associated with a particular division, function or product line.

Discretionary Expense
Expenses that can be adjusted in the short term. Examples include salaries, production wages, employee benefits, advertising, and supplies. Typically account for about two-thirds of total period expenses.

Dividends
Distributions of net earnings of the business to the shareholders/owners.

Dollar Volume of Sales
The dollar amount of goods or services sold to customers. Amount of sales that a business is likely to achieve can be determined by multiplying the average turnover by the capital invested in the business.

Earnings per Share
Net income of the business divided by the number of shares outstanding. Represents the dollar amount of earnings allocable to each shareholder.

Equipment
Physical goods used in a business, such as machinery, computers and furniture.

Equity
Equal to the capital invested in the business by the owners plus the accumulated earnings of the business that have not been paid out to the owners.

Generally Accepted Accounting Principles (GAAP)
The conventions, rules and procedures defined by the Financial Accounting Standards Board as proper accounting practices.

Gross Margin
Difference between sales and variable costs. Or, how much is left after the variable costs are subtracted from the sales.

Gross Profit
Difference between sales and cost of goods sold. Or, how much is left after the costs of goods sold are subtracted from sales.

Income Statement
Part of the financial statement that tells you how much your income has been for a period of time; what all of your costs and expenses have been and how much is left over as profit on the bottom line.

Interest
The amount paid to debtors for the use of their capital. Represents the cost of debt capital.

Inventory
The amount of product on hand to be sold to customers (finished goods inventory), currently being manufactured (work in process inventory) or to be used in production (raw material inventory).

Liabilities
Amounts owed by the business to its suppliers and debtors. Includes accounts payable and debt.

Marketplace
All existing and potential customers.

Net Earnings (also Net Income or Net Profit)
The sum remaining after all expenses, including taxes, have been deducted from sales.

Payables
    See Accounts Payable

Percent to Sales
Fraction or amount determined relative to the dollar volume of sales. To express an amount as a percent to sales, simply divide that amount by the dollar volume of sales. For instance, if sales are $1,000,000, and gross margin is $400,000, then the gross margin percent to sales is 40%.

Period Expenses
Expenses that are time oriented as opposed to volume oriented; do not change in direct proportion to a change in sales volume but change gradually over a period of time in response to new levels of output, either higher or lower. Examples include depreciation, rent, property taxes, salaries, travel and utilities.

Physical Turnover
How many days supply of inventory are on hand. Calculated by dividing cost of goods sold by inventory.

Profit
The compensation accruing to the entrepreneur for the assumption of risk.

Rate of Return
Profit or net earnings received and expressed as a percent of the investment. Also called Return on Investment.

Receivables
    See Accounts Receivable

Return on Invested Capital (ROIC)
Measurement of the profitability of a business expressed as a percentage of the capital invested. Calculated by dividing Net Profit before Interest Expense by Total Capital. Provides the most accurate measurement of profitability of a business because it is tied to the total amount of capital invested in the business. Also provides a more accurate comparison of profitability among different businesses or investments.

Return on Sales
Net earnings divided by the dollar volume of sales. Represents the net return to the business based on the volume of business sold.

Revenue
   See Dollar Volume of Sales

Sales
   See Dollar Volume of Sales

Turnover
Represents how frequently a dollar invested in the business generates sales revenue. Computed as Sales divided by Capital. Turnover depends on the nature of the business, limits the attainable sales volume of the business, and determines the rate of return required on sales.

Value Added
Represents the value of a business's product or service to its customers above its cost. Technology generally has a high value add, as the customer cannot create such technology for himself, whereas distribution generally has a lower value add, as it is simply a convenience of moving product from one location to another.

Variable Costs & Expenses
Determined by the behavior of costs and expenses and how they will react under changing conditions of production and sales. Variable costs will increase or decrease in direct proportion to dollar volume of sales. Examples include cost of materials used in production or purchased for resale, labor costs, warranty expenses, commissions. Always volume oriented.

INDEX

A

Accounts Payable, 116
Accounts Receivable, 116
Accumulated Earnings, 116
Administration, 66
Annualized, 116
Assets, 19, 23, 25, 116

B

Balance Sheet, 10–41
    adjusting points of control on, 80–81
    Capital on, 10–12
    Cash on, 33–34
    and control of Capital, 15–25
    defined, 116
    and Five Percent Control Report, 74, 77
    five percent management of, 30–31
    Inventory on, 37
    Payables on, 19–20, 38–40
    and Percent to Sales, 23–25
    Receivables on, 34–36
    and turnover, 12–14
    uses of, 71, 77
Before-tax return, 62

C

Capital, 10–12
    Debt Capital, 11
    defined, 11, 116
    and division/product line profitability, 94–100
    Equity Capital, 11
    on Five Percent Control Report, 74–77
    gradual liquidation of, 101–102
    as limit on Sales, 11–12
    management/control of, 15–40
    operating costs and slippage in, 91
    and Payables, 19
    as Percent to Sales, 23–25
    pretax cost of, 62
    return on, 61, 62 (*See also* Return on Capital)
    Total, 18

and turnover, 12–14
turnover for, 21–22
Cash, 18, 33–34
as Percent to Sales, 23, 25
turnover for, 21
Cash Flow, 33, 116
Changes, adjusting for, 77–92
on Five Percent Control Report, 89–91
in Inventory, 78–91
Commissions, 46
Committed Expenses, 64–67, 116
Cost of Capital, 61, 62, 116
Cost of doing business, 58, 101
Cost of Goods Sold, 37, 117

D

Days Sales Outstanding, 117
Debt, 117
Debt Capital, 11
Depreciation, 117
Detail, 8–9
Direct Costs, 117
Discounts, 46
Discretionary Expenses, 64, 67, 68
defined, 117
offsetting Inventory increase with, 88–89
Dividends, 117
Divisions, profitability of, 93–100
Dollar Volume of Sales, 14, 44, 46, 117

E

Earnings per Share, 117
Equipment, 18, 38
defined, 117
as Percent to Sales, 23, 25
turnover for, 21
Equity, 11, 117
Expenses. *See also* Period Expenses; Variable Costs & Expenses
Committed, 64–67, 116
Discretionary, 64, 67, 68, 88–89, 117
and division/product line profitability, 94–100
Warranty, 46

F

Financial statements, 74. *See also specific statements*
Financial turnover, 37

Five Percent Control Report, 72–77
    and adjustment for Inventory increase, 89–91
    Balance Sheet control points for, 107–108
    completion of, 112
    constructing, 105–114
    and emphasis on future, 92
    Income Statement information for, 109–110
    Return on Capital determination for, 111
    selection of financial statements for, 106
Five percent management, 3–10
    of Balance Sheet, 30–31
    and detail, 8–9
    of Income Statement, 43
    and success in business, 5–7
Five percent rule, 9
    in adjusting for changes, 77–92
    for Balance Sheet, 10–41
    for divisional or product line analysis, 93–100
    for Income Statement, 42–71
Freight Out, 46

G

Generally Accepted Accounting Principles (GAAP), vii–viii, 117
Gross Margin, 51–54
    defined, 118
    Percent to Sales, 51–54
    and Variable Costs, 51–54
Gross Profit, 118
Gross Sales, 46

I

Imputed cost, 58
Income Statement, 10, 42–71
    adjusting points of control on, 80–81
    defined, 118
    Dollar Volume of Sales, 44, 46
    and Five Percent Control Report, 74, 77
    Gross Margin, 51–54
    and offset for Inventory increase, 86–87
    Period Expenses, 47–50, 55, 63–68
    and Profit, 55–63
    and turnover rate, 26
    uses of, 71, 77
    Variable Costs & Expenses, 44–48
Interest, 118
Inventory, 18, 37

adjusting for changes in, 78–91
defined, 118
as Percent to Sales, 23, 25
turnover for, 21, 37

J

Judgment, 93

L

Labor costs, 45
Liabilities, 38, 118
Longer-term profitability, 93

M

Marketplace, 118
Materials costs, 45

N

Net Earnings (Net Income, Net Profit), 118
Net Sales, 46

O

Operating costs, 91

P

Payables, 18, 38–40. *See also* Accounts Payable
    offsetting Inventory increase with, 81, 83
    as Percent to Sales, 23, 25
    turnover of, 21, 38–40
Percent to Sales
    Capital groups in, 23–25
    defined, 118
    Gross Margin, 51–54
    Period Expenses as, 49
Period Expenses, 47–50, 55, 63–68
    Committed, 64–67
    defined, 118
    Discretionary, 64, 67, 68
    as Percent to Sales, 49
Physical Turnover, 37, 118
Plant and Equipment, 21, 38. *See also* Equipment
Pretax cost of Capital, 62
Price increases, 91
Production
    as Committed Expense, 66
    Variable Costs of, 45, 46
Product lines, profitability of, 93–100

Profit, vii–viii, 55–63. *See also* Profit required
    as cost of doing business, 101
    definitions of, 30, 56–58, 119
    on Five Percent Control Report, 74–77
Profitability
    of divisions or product lines, 93–100
    longer-term, 93
Profit required, 26–30
    as percent Return on Capital, 62
    and Period Expenses allowed, 55
    and rate of return, 61–62
    and Return on Capital, 101–102
    and taxes, 62

R

Rate of Return
    on Capital (*See* Return on Capital)
    defined, 119
    and Profit required, 61–62
    and risk, 58–60
Receivables, 18, 34–36. *See also* Accounts Receivable
    offsetting Inventory increase with, 81–82
    as Percent to Sales, 23, 25
    turnover for, 21, 34–36
Reports, 10, 71–72. *See also specific reports, e.g.:* Income Statement
Return on Capital, 61
    control of, 91–92
    maintaining goal for, 81
    Profit required as percent of, 62
    requirement for, 101–102
Return on Invested Capital (ROIC), viii, 119
Return on Investment, 27–28
Return on Sales, 119
Returns & Allowances, 46
Revenue. *See* Dollar Volume of Sales
Risk, rate of return and, 58–61
ROIC. *See* Return on Invested Capital
Rolling projection, twelve-month, 92
Royalties, 46

S

Sales
    Capital and limit on, 11–12
    Capital groups as percent of, 23–25
    as Committed Expense, 66
    Dollar Volume of (*See* Dollar Volume of Sales)

      and Gross Margin, 51
      and Profit required, 26–30
      and turnover, 12–14
      Variable Costs of, 45–47
Sales Potential, 13–14
Selling prices, 91
Success in business, 5–7, 77

T

Taxes, Profit required and, 62
Terms of sale, 36
Total Assets, 23, 25
Total Capital, 18
Turnover
      for Capital, 12–14, 21–22
      for Cash, 21
      defined, 119
      for five groups in use of Capital, 20–25
      for Inventory, 21, 37
      of money, 37
      for Payables, 21, 38–40
      physical vs. financial, 37
      for Plant & Equipment, 21
      and profit rate on sales, 27–30
      reason for calculating, 26
      for Receivables, 21, 34–36
      and type of business, 14
Twelve-month rolling projection, 92

V

Value Added, 119
Variable Costs & Expenses, 44–48, 119
      and Gross Margin, 51–54
      of Production, 45, 46
      of Sales, 45–47

W

Warranty Expenses, 46
WorldCom, viii

If you have enjoyed this book and would like to order more of Carole A. Symonds' works:

Millionaire Manager Profit Management Training Simplified (CDs)
Millionaire Manager Talks to Wall Street
Millionaire Manager Fights Inflation

please visit our website at: www.MillionaireManager.com.

If you would like to order more of Curtis W. Symonds' works:

Basic Financial Management
Profit Dollars and Earnings Sense
Pricing for Profit
Administracion Financiera Basica
Administracion De Las Utilidades
Suplemento Las Utilidades En Epocas De Inflation

please visit our website at: www.GlobalFinancialPublishing.com.

About the Authors

CAROLE A. SYMONDS, CPA, MST, is a Partner with one of the world's most prestigious Big Four Public Accouting Firms. Named to the *Boston Business Journal's* Top 40 Under 40 list of Greater Boston's next generation of business leaders and innovators, Carole has over 12 years of experience working with clients in the manufacturing, wholesale, retail and service industries. Carole obtained a Master of Science in Taxation from Northeastern University, has been an associate professor at Thomas College in their Master's program, and is a featured lecturer on corporate taxation and financial matters.

Prior to her partnership, Carole was a member of the Washington National Tax Services Practice, consulting with multinational clients on an array of federal taxation issues.

CURTIS W. SYMONDS has advised such distinguished corporations and agencies as DuPont, Kennecott Copper, J.C. Penney, GTE, Tektronix, John Hancock, Dravo, Air-France, A.C. Neilsen, Arthur D. Little, The Jim Pattison Group, Creative Playthings, Borg Warner, Harrah's, Allied Chemical, U.S. Post Office, Teledyne, and numerous small and medium-sized companies here in the United States and abroad.

The concepts and measurements contained in this book have been presented in lecture form at many seminars and universities for the Young Presidents Organization, the American Management Association and numerous trade and professional organizations around the world.

Mr. Symonds's published works on the subject of financial management include *Basic Financial Management, Managing Profits Under Inflation, Profit Dollars and Earnings Sense, A Design for Business Intelligence,* and *Pricing for Profit.*

Please share this book with others.

LaVergne, TN USA
21 February 2010
173782LV00004B/5/A